How a Bill
Becomes a Law

Tracie Egan

Primary Source

The Rosen Publishing Group, Inc., New York

Published in 2004 by The Rosen Publishing Group, Inc.
29 East 21st Street, New York, NY 10010

Copyright © 2004 by The Rosen Publishing Group, Inc.

First Edition

Library of Congress Cataloging-in-Publication Data

Egan, Tracie.
How a bill becomes a law/Tracie Egan.—1st ed.
    p. cm.—(A primary source library of American citizenship)
Summary: Discusses how legislators devise, debate, and approve new laws, with the concurrence of the president.
ISBN 0-8239-4471-9 (lib. bdg.)
1. Legislation—United States—Juvenile literature. 2. United States. Congress—Juvenile literature. [1. Legislation.]
I. Title. II. Series.
KF4945.Z9E38 2004
328.73'077—dc22
                                                                                                2003015579

Manufactured in the United States of America

On the cover: Bottom left: In the East Room of the White House, President George Bush signs into law his tax cut package in 2003. Top right: A view of the Capitol and central Washington, from a lithograph published in 1871. Background: The text of the Civil Rights Act of 1964.

Photo credits: cover (background), p. 29 (left) © Enrolled Acts and Resolutions of Congress, 1789–, General Records of the United States Government, Record Group 11, National Archives; cover (top right), p. 5 © Library of Congress, Geography and Map Division; cover (bottom left), pp. 8, 11 (top), 17, 18, 19, 20, 22, 23, 24, 26, 28, 29 (right), 30 © AP/Wide World Photo; pp. 4, 11 (bottom), 15, 16 © Bettmann/Corbis; p. 7 © Wally McNamee; p. 9 courtesy of the United States Representatives; p. 10 © Corbis; p. 13 courtesy of the United States Government Printing Office; p. 21 © Library of Congress, Prints and Photographs; p. 25 © 2003 Picture History, LLC.

Designer: Tahara Hasan

Contents

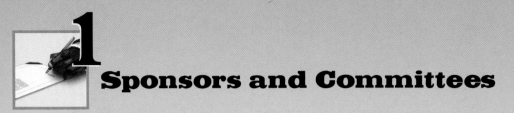

1 Sponsors and Committees

Laws are created by the members of Congress. When a member of the House of Representatives or the Senate has an idea for a new law, he or she becomes the sponsor for that law. The sponsor introduces the law in the form of a bill to the rest of Congress. That bill must go through a process of approval before it can become a law.

In 1932, President Herbert Hoover speaks to a joint session of Congress. These are the men and women in the House of Representatives and the Senate who make the laws.

VIEW OF WASHINGTON CITY.

A view of the Capitol in a lithograph published in 1871. The House of Representatives and the Senate meet in opposite wings of the building.

If the bill was proposed by a member of the House of Representatives, it is assigned a number, printed out, and given to each representative. The Speaker of the House then assigns the bill to a committee so that it may be studied. Committees are different groups of congresspeople who have authority over different functions of government.

Sponsorship

Bills may be sponsored by more than one member of Congress. Some bills have many sponsors. This is a way for members of Congress to demonstrate their support for a bill.

Senator William Roth of Delaware, cosponsor of the Roth-Kemp tax-cutting bill, stands before an elephant, the symbol of the Republican Party, and drums up support for his legislation.

The committee hears testimonies from experts about the effects of the bill. The committee then has three options. It can vote to release the bill with a recommendation to pass it. This is called reporting it out. The committee can also revise the bill before releasing it. The committee can also lay the bill aside and postpone any discussion of it. Laying a bill aside is called tabling and often means a bill will never become a law.

During a morning staff meeting, Representative Marty Meehan of Massachusetts discusses the campaign finance reform law he cosponsored that is about to be debated in the House of Representatives.

HEARING

BEFORE THE

SUBCOMMITTEE ON
OVERSIGHT AND INVESTIGATIONS

OF THE

COMMITTEE ON ENERGY AND COMMERCE
HOUSE OF REPRESENTATIVES

ONE HUNDRED SEVENTH CONGRESS

SECOND SESSION

FEBRUARY 7, 2002

Serial No. 107–88

Printed for the use of the Committee on Energy and Commerce

Available via the World Wide Web: http://www.access.gpo.gov/congress/house

U.S. GOVERNMENT PRINTING OFFICE
77–987CC   WASHINGTON : 2002

For sale by the Superintendent of Documents, U.S. Government Printing Office
Internet: bookstore.gpo.gov   Phone: toll free (866) 512–1800; DC area (202) 512–1800
Fax: (202) 512–2250   Mail: Stop SSOP, Washington, DC 20402–0001

The printed minutes of a hearing held by a committee of the House of Representatives on the Enron financial scandal in 2002. After such hearings and investigations, Congress proposes a law, which is printed as a bill, and after passage by Congress, the bill becomes an act.

These decisions about what to do with a bill are often influenced by the chairperson of the committee, who is elected by the majority of the committee members. The chairperson therefore enjoys the support of the majority of the committee and can count on the majority to back his or her decisions. Committee chairpersons have a lot of political power.

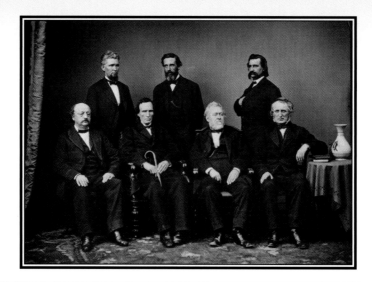

The members of the House committee who voted to impeach President Andrew Johnson in 1868. The House impeaches (that is, brings charges against a president), and the Senate decides the merit of those charges and determines the punishment.

In 2003, Representative Edith Clark was the chairperson of the Health and Human Services Subcommittee of the House of Representatives. Committee chairpersons are very powerful and can often make or break legislation. Below, in 1951, Lyndon B. Johnson *(left)* discusses a bill to draft eighteen-year-olds with other members of the Senate Armed Services Committee.

If a bill is reported out, a committee report is written. The report describes the purpose of the bill and lists the reasons why the committee thinks the bill should be passed. The bill then goes on the calendar. The calendar is a list of bills waiting to be passed. Now the House Rules Committee decides if the bill will be voted upon quickly, debated, or amended.

Committee Records

The government prints transcripts of testimonies made by experts and interested parties during committee hearings on a bill, and these transcripts are made available to any citizen interested in reading them.

106TH CONGRESS
1ST SESSION

H. R. 1

To provide for Social Security reform.

IN THE HOUSE OF REPRESENTATIVES

MARCH 1, 1999

Mr. HASTERT introduced the following bill; which was referred to the
Committee on Ways and Means

A BILL

To provide for Social Security reform.

1   *Be it enacted by the Senate and House of Representa-*

2 *tives of the United States of America in Congress assembled,*

3 **SECTION 1. FINDINGS.**

4   The Congress finds that—

5   (1) the President, in his 1998 State of the

6   Union address, committed the Nation to saving So-

7   cial Security, a call which he repeated in his 1999

8   State of the Union address;

9   (2) recognizing the importance of Social Secu-

10   rity to millions of American families, Speaker

11   Hastert at the opening of the 106th Congress re-

12   served the House bill designation H.R. 1 for the

A page from the printed version of a bill, a law proposed for consideration by Congress. The information at the top indicates that it was the first bill proposed in the House of Representatives for the 106th session of Congress in 1999.

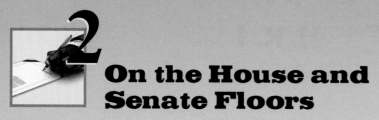

2 On the House and Senate Floors

The bill then goes to the floor of the House of Representatives for consideration. There is a complete reading of the bill. The merits of the bill are debated. The members of the House of Representatives then vote on the bill, and if the bill receives a majority of the votes, it moves to the Senate.

Filibustering

Sometimes members of Congress try to prevent the passing of a bill by filibustering. Filibustering occurs when those who oppose a bill give long speeches before the Senate. Because there is no limit to the amount of time the Senate can debate a bill, the hope is that supporters will withdraw a bill or give in on key points after enduring hours of dull speeches.

In 1954, Senator Albert Gore of Tennessee, the father of former vice president Al Gore, reenacts a filibuster he conducted on the Senate floor for more than ten hours to block a bill he did not approve of.

When a bill moves to the Senate, it is again assigned to a committee. The Senate committee studies the bill and either releases or tables it. If the bill is released, it goes to the Senate floor. The bill is debated and then the senators cast their votes. A simple majority of fifty-one votes is all that is needed for the bill to be passed.

This 1940 photo shows the Senate debating a bill. A limited space above the Senate chamber is open for the public to listen to the debates.

In 1958, Lieutenant General James H. Doolittle *(right)* testifies before a Senate committee on the need for civilian control of the American space program. Congress often hears the testimony of experts before deciding what kind of law it will create.

Once the bill is passed by the House of Representatives and the Senate, it is referred to a conference committee. A conference committee is made up of members from both houses of Congress. The committee works out the differences between the two versions of the bill passed by the House of Representatives and the Senate. The bill is then sent back to both houses of Congress for final approval.

Members of the House and Senate Banking Committees meet in conference to discuss different versions of a budget proposal in 1995.

Members of the House-Senate Commerce Committee discuss legislation about prescription drug benefits for seniors.

Once the bill receives the final approval of the House and the Senate, it is printed by the Government Printing Office. This is called enrolling. The clerk from the House who first introduced the bill must certify it. The enrolled bill is signed by the Speaker of the House, and then the vice president, who presides over the Senate.

In 1999, Speaker of the House Dennis Hastert *(center left)* and Senate majority leader Trent Lott *(center right)* celebrate passage of a bill that will simplify rules for schools to apply for federal funding. The bill became a law when President Bill Clinton signed it.

This photograph of the machine shop at the U.S. Government Printing Office was taken in the 1930s. This office prints all public laws and records of congressional activities.

3 The President's Approval

After the enrolled bill receives the signatures of the Speaker of the House and the vice president, it has one more step before it can become a law. It must be approved by the president. The president has ten days to sign or veto the bill. If the president signs the bill, then it officially becomes a law.

With Vice President Al Gore looking on, President Bill Clinton signs into law a bill creating a new national park in Utah. The signing ceremony was held at the edge of the Grand Canyon in Arizona.

In the Oval Office of the White House, with Speaker of the House Dennis Hastert *(left)* looking on, President George W. Bush signs a bill into law.

If the president chooses to veto, or not sign, the bill, it still has a chance to become a law. The vetoed bill can be sent back to Congress to be voted on again or changed to satisfy the president's objections. After a presidential veto, a bill needs two-thirds of the Senate and two-thirds of the House to vote in favor of the bill in order for it to become a law without the president's signature.

This is the document President Bill Clinton signed in 1997 to veto portions of the budget bill submitted to him by Congress. Clinton was the first president to use the line item veto, which allows a president to veto certain parts of a bill.

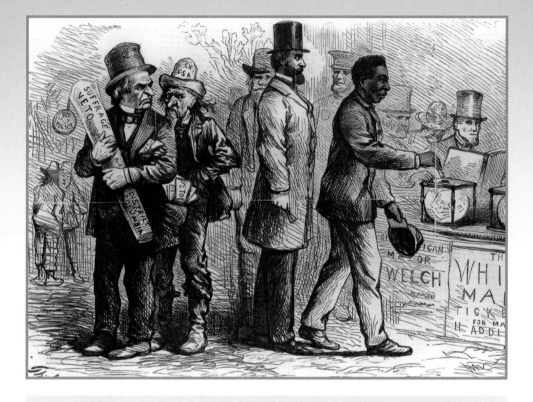

This cartoon by Thomas Nast from *Harper's Weekly* in 1867 shows African Americans voting in an election, with President Andrew Johnson on the left turning away from them and holding in his hands a bill to deprive them of the right to vote.

The process for creating a new law may seem lengthy, but there is a reason for this. It is important for each member of Congress to carefully consider a bill before approving it. By doing so, these elected officials ensure that the voices of the people who voted for them are heard.

President John F. Kennedy signs a bill providing equal pay to women. Giving away the pens used to sign bills into law to supporters of the legislation has become a presidential tradition.

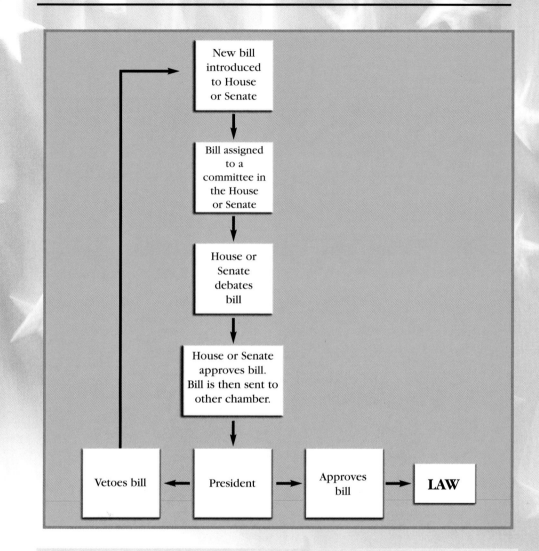

New bill
introduced
to House
or Senate

↓

Bill assigned
to a
committee in
the House
or Senate

↓

House or
Senate
debates
bill

↓

House or Senate
approves bill.
Bill is then sent to
other chamber.

↓

Vetoes bill ← President → Approves bill → **LAW**

This flow chart shows how a proposed law works its way through Congress and then goes to the president. If vetoed, it goes back to Congress for reconsideration.

Even after a bill becomes a law, it may be invalidated by the judicial system. The courts must decide if the new law conforms to the provisions of the Constitution, our fundamental law. They decide this if someone is convicted of violating the new law and appeals his or her conviction.

Senators Christopher Dodd *(left)* and Charles Schumer give a press conference before the steps of the Supreme Court Building in Washington, where they defended a bill granting extended family leave to state employees that was challenged in the Court.

H. R. 7152   PUBLIC LAW 88-352

Eighty-eighth Congress of the United States of America

AT THE SECOND SESSION

Begun and held at the City of Washington on Tuesday, the seventh day of January, one thousand nine hundred and sixty-four

An Act

To enforce the constitutional right to vote, to confer jurisdiction upon the district courts of the United States to provide injunctive relief against discrimination in public accommodations, to authorize the Attorney General to institute suits to protect constitutional rights in public facilities and public education, to extend the Commission on Civil Rights, to prevent discrimination in federally assisted programs, to establish a Commission on Equal Employment Opportunity, and for other purposes.

Be it enacted by the Senate and House of Representatives of the United States of America in Congress assembled, That this Act may be cited as the "Civil Rights Act of 1964".

TITLE I—VOTING RIGHTS

SEC. 101. Section 2004 of the Revised Statutes (42 U.S.C. 1971), as amended by section 131 of the Civil Rights Act of 1957 (71 Stat. 637), and as further amended by section 601 of the Civil Rights Act of 1960 (74 Stat. 90), is further amended as follows:

(a) Insert "1" after "(a)" in subsection (a) and add at the end of subsection (a) the following new paragraphs:

"(2) No person acting under color of law shall—

"(A) in determining whether any individual is qualified under State law or laws to vote in any Federal election, apply any standard, practice, or procedure different from the standards, practices, or procedures applied under such law or laws to other individuals within the same county, parish, or similar political subdivision who have been found by State officials to be qualified to vote;

"(B) deny the right of any individual to vote in any Federal election because of an error or omission on any record or paper relating to any application, registration, or other act requisite to voting, if such error or omission is not material in determining whether such individual is qualified under State law to vote in such election; or

"(C) employ any literacy test as a qualification for voting in any Federal election unless (i) such test is administered to each individual and is conducted wholly in writing, and (ii) a certified copy of the test and of the answers given by the individual is furnished to him within twenty-five days of the submission of his request made within the period of time during which records and papers are required to be retained and preserved pursuant to title III of the Civil Rights Act of 1960 (42 U.S.C. 1974–74e; 74 Stat. 88) : *Provided, however,* That the Attorney General may enter into agreements with appropriate State or local authorities that preparation, conduct, and maintenance of such tests in accordance with the provisions of applicable State or local law, including such special provisions as are necessary in the preparation, conduct, and maintenance of such tests for persons who are blind or otherwise physically handicapped, meet the purposes of this subparagraph and constitute compliance therewith.

"(3) For purposes of this subsection—

"(A) the term 'vote' shall have the same meaning as in subsection (e) of this section;

"(B) the phrase 'literacy test' includes any test of the ability to read, write, understand, or interpret any matter."

(b) Insert immediately following the period at the end of the first sentence of subsection (c) the following new sentence: "If in any such proceeding literacy is a relevant fact there shall be a rebuttable

Above, the title page of the Civil Rights Act of 1964, first proposed by John F. Kennedy and signed into law by President Lyndon B. Johnson after Kennedy's assassination. Below, in 1956, Rosa Parks was put on trial for sitting at the front of a Montgomery, Alabama, city bus, an incident that caused the passage of the Civil Rights Act.

That appeal may be taken as far as the U.S. Supreme Court. The Supreme Court is the final authority on the constitutionality of laws passed by Congress. If the Supreme Court finds the law to be constitutional, it will stay in effect until Congress passes another law to change or cancel it.

The Supreme Court Building in Washington, D.C. Ultimately, the justices of the Supreme Court decide the validity of laws by comparing them to the Constitution.

Glossary

amend (uh-MEND) To improve or make better by making changes.

authority (uh-THOR-ih-tee) The power to command or enforce laws; when someone is in charge.

certification (sur-tih-fi-KAY-shun) A confirmation or acknowledgement in writing.

Congress (KON-gres) The elected members of the House of Representatives and the Senate.

debate (dih-BAYT) A formal discussion between people with different views.

majority (muh-JOR-ih-tee) More than half.

representative (reh-prih-ZEN-tuh-tiv) A person in the government who is chosen by the public through popular vote.

sponsor (SPON-sor) The person who urges the passing of a certain bill.

testimony (TES-tuh-moh-nee) Evidence or facts given by a person.

veto (VEE-toh) To reject a bill by not signing it.

Web Sites

Due to the changing nature of Internet links, the Rosen Publishing Group, Inc., has developed an online list of Web sites related to the subject of this book. This site is updated regularly. Please use this link to access the list:

http://www.rosenlinks.com/pslac/hbbl

Primary Source Image List

Page 4: President Hoover and Congress, photographed on February 22, 1932, in Washington, D.C.
Page 5: *The Capitol*, printed by E. Sachse & Company of Baltimore, 1871, now with the Library of Congress.
Page 7: Senator William Roth, photographed by Wally McNamee in 1978.
Page 8: Representative Marty Meehan, photographed by Kenneth Lambert for the Associated Press, 2001.
Page 9: Hearing before the Subcommittee on Oversight and Investigations, February 7, 2002; available from the U.S. Government Printing Office.
Page 10: The Johnson impeachment committee, photographed by Mathew Brady, 1868.

Page 11 (top): Representative Edith Clark, photographed by George Lane for the Associated Press, 2003.
Page 11 (bottom): Lyndon Johnson, 1951.
Page 13: House of Representatives bill H. R. 1, 106th session of Congress, 1999.
Page 15: Senator Albert Gore, photographed by Al Muto, 1954.
Page 16: The Senate chamber, 1940.
Page 17: James Doolittle testifies before Congress, photographed for the Associated Press, 1958.
Page 18: House and Senate Banking Committees, photographed for the Associated Press, 1995.
Page 19: The House-Senate Commerce Committee, photographed by Charles Dharapak for the Associated Press, 2003.
Page 20: Dennis Hastert and Trent Lott, photographed by Dennis Cook for the Associated Press, 1999.
Page 21: U.S. Government Printing Office, photographed in the 1930s, now with the Library of Congress.
Page 22: Bill Clinton and Al Gore at the Grand Canyon, photographed by Greg Gibson for the Associated Press, 1996.
Page 23: President Bush and House Speaker Dennis Hastert, photographed by Ron Edmons for the Associated Press, 2002.
Page 24: The line item veto, photographed by Ruth Fremson for the Associated Press, 1997.
Page 25: *The Georgetown Election*, by Thomas Nast, *Harper's Weekly*, March 16, 1867.
Page 26: Kennedy signs legislation, photographed by Harvey Georges for the Associated Press, 1963.
Page 28: Senators Christopher Dodd and Charles Schumer, photographed by Evan Vucci for the Associated Press, 2003.
Page 29 (left): Civil Rights Act of 1964, now in the National Archives.
Page 29 (right): Rosa Parks, Montgomery, Alabama, 1956, photographed by Gene Herrick for the Associated Press.
Page 30: The Supreme Court Building, photographed by Ken Cedeno for the Associated Press, 2001.

 **Index**

About the Author

Tracie Egan is a freelance writer who lives in Brooklyn, New York.